Unity

ISBN: 1542538211
ISBN-13: 978-1542538213

"together we are.
   we are the stain glass of life.
   we are the delicate pieces,
   we are fluttery and light

   we are the endurance
   we are the strength.
   we are the smooth surface
   we slip, glide into place

   each of us textiles,
   a pattern,
   one whole,
   despite many distinctions
   remains a similar role

   we are a rainbow of colors,
   but remove just one,
   we are incomplete.
   like the moon
   without sun

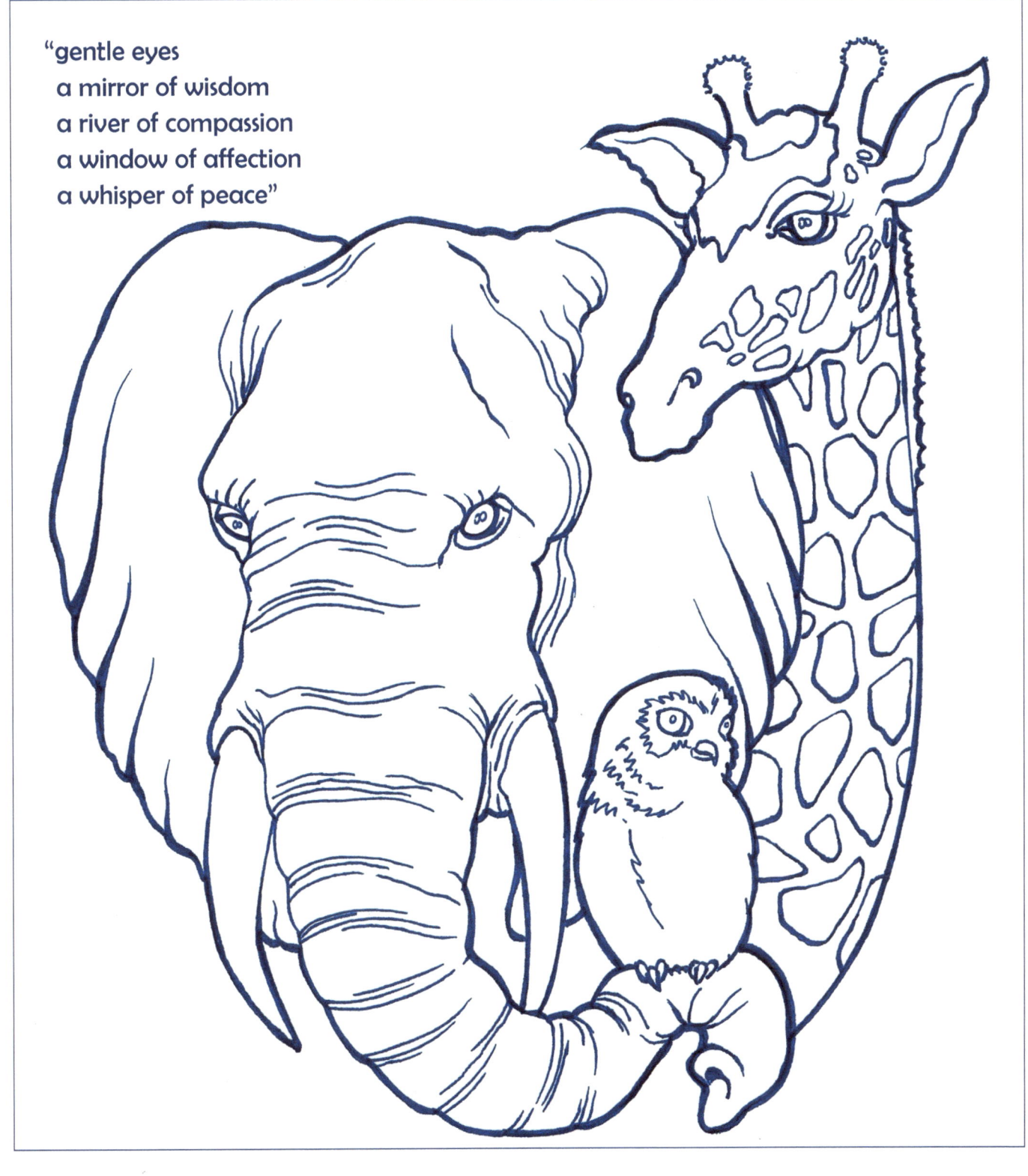

"gentle eyes
   a mirror of wisdom
   a river of compassion
   a window of affection
   a whisper of peace"

"where the land meets the sea
where the sky reaches all,
where harmony spreads
like a beckoning call,
rising and setting
like the moon and the sun,
together we flow
together as one"

"Each one of us a story.
 on our own,
 complete.
 But stories often come alive
 when they mix, and match and meet."

"we are pieces of a puzzle,
 each piece different and unique,
 but the picture's not complete,
 if you take away a piece"

"Individually,
unique.
just as remarkable,
as a whole"

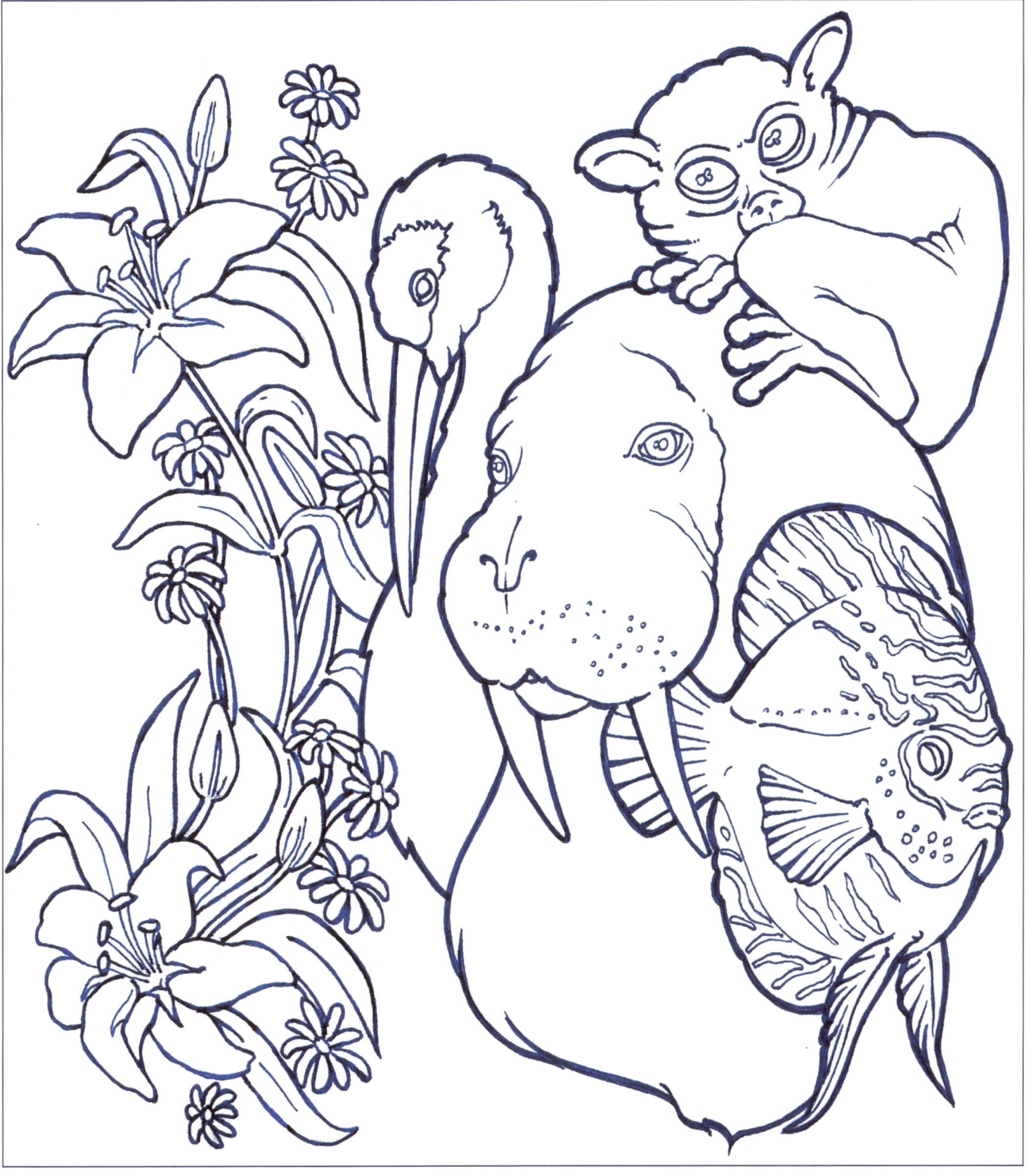

"you don't have to look,
for the features we might share.
you don't have to search,
for something that's not there.
you don't have to seek,
for resemblance in our skin.
you just need to pause,
and find the balance that's within"

"Though seemingly unfitting
to the eye that is plain,
there would be no difference
if not for separate terrains.
all that is here,
they fit like a puzzle
if not for one,
leaves an emptiness,
not subtle"

"We don't have to be the same,
to find the peace we wish to claim

www.ingramcontent.com/pod-product-compliance
Lightning Source LLC
Chambersburg PA
CBHW041516280526
45792CB00004B/1277